Unlocking, Releasing And Receiving Your Baby

Toyin Adewunmi

Unlocking, Releasing and Receiving Your Baby
Toyin Adewunmi

Unless otherwise stated, all scripture quotations are taken from
the Holy Bible, New King James Version (NKJV). Other versions
cited are NIV, KJV, GNB, God's Word and NLT.

ISBN 978-1-907734-17-5
First Edition
First Printing June 2014

Covenant Publishing
samadewunmi@btinternet.com

Covenant Publishing is part of New Covenant Church
Charity Registered in England & Wales number 1004343
Registered Address: 506-510 Old Kent Road. LONDON SE1 5BA

Cover Design by Covenant Publishing Team
Toyin Adewunmi's photo by David Adetoye
Published by Covenant Publishing
Printed in the United Kingdom

Table of Content

Table of Content

Foreword

$\mathscr{I}$ have just finished reading this excellent book and warmly recommend it not only to those who desire children but to every single person who desires to "walk on water," and for every person who desires to move mountains. This is a book about faith that looks on the impossible and says, "It can be done!"

It is a book about the word of God and its efficacy. Toyin Adewunmi writes with clarity and grace. It is a compelling read and a profound read. It has the possibility to be a life-changing read. Toyin, I salute you. May this book go far and wide.

Kate Jinadu
Pastor, New Covenant Church
Director LIBERTY – making people free

Preface

The idea to write this book came to me in a dream about eight years ago when I was given a title: *unlocking, releasing and receiving your baby*. I immediately got up from my sleep to write it down so I would not forget. Initially, I was not particularly excited about the title because I already had another script that was to follow my first book. However, somehow, I found that I could not proceed with 'my' almost ready script without thinking of "unlocking, releasing and receiving your baby." In due course, I realised that God was up to something, and knew this book must be written before any other book I had in mind. Eventually, I made a start with the book about five years ago.

Since the time I received the title in my dream, I have had to reflect over it on numerous occasions. This stirred up several questions in me, such as: why do couples have to unlock and release the blessing of the womb before they could receive their babies? Did God not pronounce the blessing of fruitfulness upon mankind in the Garden of Eden? Besides, many have received their babies without having to unlock or release anything, why should some have to? These questions ran through my mind many times. You may also be asking yourself these questions.

Many people who are diagnosed with a medical condition may not necessarily think their health problem has a spiritual origin. To such category of people, the idea of children locked away seems somewhat ridiculous. The ludicrous search for a key or code, which they were not even aware was lost, in order to unlock the innocent babies may seem useless. Why would you spiritualise a medical problem? And, by the way, who locked the babies away and where are they locked?

I had been through a similar experience, and can still remember a few of the questions that ran through my mind when infertility was seen through spiritual lenses. The Bible says in John 10:10 that:

"The thief does not come except to steal, and to kill, and to destroy. I have come that they may have life, and that they may have it more abundantly."

This passage describes the threefold operation of the devil: to kill, steal and destroy. Believe me; he will not do anything short of these three. Given the permission, he would go beyond his boundary, and that is why the Lord warned him concerning Job's life.

> *"'And the Lord said to Satan, behold all that he has is in your power; only do not lay a hand on his person'"* (Job 1:12).

The fact that people do not have an understanding of the way Satan operates does not negate what he is capable of doing. It is generally thought that what is unknown would not harm or hurt. Whereas this may be true to some extent, it is not however, always the case. The Bible also tells us in Hosea 4:6,

> *"My people are destroyed for lack of knowledge."*

Sadly, for some people, the blessing of the womb has been stolen and locked away without their knowledge or consent. In a vision that God showed to me, I saw babies locked away in a house. The enemy, for one reason or another, was obstructing the release of their babies. However, they could be unlocked and released by the power of the Almighty God.

> *"For this purpose the Son of God was manifested, that He might destroy the works of the devil"* (1 John 3:8b).

I do not know how the enemy has tried to steal, kill or destroy your children; maybe through several miscarriages, abortions, stillbirths, gynaecological problems that would not allow fertility to take place. I have come to announce to you, by the power of the Holy Spirit, that Jesus Christ came that you may have life, carry life, and give birth to as many children as God wants.

> *"But I have come that they may have life and that they may have it more abundantly."* (John 10:10b).

As the title implies, this book is written for couples trusting God for the fruit of the womb. However, the biblical principles and insights shared in this book could also be adapted to any other challenging situations that people might be facing.

Acknowledgements

I give all the glory to God the Father, Son and Holy Spirit for counting me worthy to be a vessel fit for this purpose; this is another demonstration of Your grace. Thank you, Lord for using my hands as your pen; to inscribe your word on tablet of hearts. Thank you for conveying Your Mind to this little mind of mine and for opening my eyes to see beyond the ordinary. Indubitably, you are the All-powerful. I am eternally grateful.

My appreciation goes to my spiritual mother, Rev. (Mrs) Kate Jinadu from whom I learnt humility and righteous living. You have positively influenced my life. Thank you for taking time to write the foreword to this book. I appreciate and celebrate you.

My appreciation also goes to my mom, Mrs Marian Olude, who showed me from a tender age the power of prayer and the grace to be consistent in the place of prayer, thank you, mom. I love you dearly and celebrate you.

I acknowledge the support of my husband, Rev. Sam O. Adewunmi, for your encouragement and support in proofreading as well as publishing this book. Thank you for believing in me. You are one in a million, darling and I love you.

To my children, thanks for your support and persevering through the writing of this book. I love you, my darlings.

Be blessed.

With all my love.

Toyin Adewunmi

Introduction

The book, Unlocking, Releasing and Receiving your Baby, is written because the title was given to me in a dream. It is intended for couples with delay in childbearing - to encourage, comfort, challenge, and give biblical insights as well as share practical advice that will bless them. Also, the biblical principles and insights shared in this book will be a blessing to all, as they can be applied to other challenging situations as well.

I will share biblical truths that God revealed to me from different perspectives, which will bring about the manifestation of the miracle of the blessing of the womb.

Firstly, there is an unexplainable power in the word of God that can help to unlock, release, and receive what God has promised. The power in God's promises can only be unleashed through affirming His word. This is the key to unlocking the door of your blessing. Listen with your heart. You do not need to look too far to get the key. It is right there in your hand. It is the word of God - so active, living and powerful.

"But what does it say? "The word is near you, in your mouth and in your heart" (that is, the word of faith which we preach)"
(Romans 10:8).

"For the word of God is living and powerful, and sharper than any two-edged sword, piercing even to the division of soul and spirit, and of joints and marrow, and is a discerner of the thoughts and intents of the heart"
(Hebrews 4:12).

Read more about the power of God's word in Chapters 2 & 3.

Secondly, faith is a crucial element in unlocking, releasing, and receiving your baby - faith in the word of God coupled with the individual's affirmation and attestation. Affirmation of God's word through confession charges the faith battery such that impossible becomes possible. You speak, you hear, and you have faith.

"Faith comes by hearing and hearing by the word of God" (Romans 10:17).

Read more about faith in Chapter 4.

Thirdly, the power of praise cannot be over-emphasised. Praise has the power to lay hold of the key, and unlock the door. Praise releases joy, peace and unimaginable gifts from above. Praise has the power to bring down the walls of Jericho. Praise will disarm and disband the enemy set in procession against you. Praise has the power to open your eyes of understanding. It is the key that will help to unlock every door of favour, release divine blessing, and receive the unattainable.

> *"Bless the LORD, O my soul; and all that is within me, bless His holy name! Bless the LORD, O my soul, and forget not all His benefits: Who forgives all your iniquities, Who heals all your diseases, Who redeems your life from destruction, Who crowns you with loving-kindness and tender mercies, Who satisfies your mouth with good things, so that your youth is renewed like the eagle's"*
>
> (Psalm 103:1-5).

Read more about the power of praise, implications of complaining and benefits of praise in Chapters 5 & 6.

Fourthly, the name of Jesus Christ is unparalleled to any other name. The Bible confirms that the name of Jesus Christ is greater than any other.

"Therefore God also has highly exalted Him and given Him the name which is above every name" (Philippians 2:9).

Read more about the person of Jesus Christ and the power in His name in Chapters 7 & 8.

Fifthly, the power in the blood of Jesus over infertility, any disease or illness cannot be overlooked. The bible records in 1 John 5:8,

"And there are three that bear witness on earth: the Spirit, the water, and the blood; and these three agree as one."

Read more about the power in the blood in Chapters 9 & 10.

Finally, the Holy Spirit is the Senior Partner in every situation we find ourselves.

Read more about how you can partner with Him in Chapter 11.

God's power is released through His Word, faith, praise, the name of Jesus Christ, His shed blood, and the Holy Spirit. My prayer is that as you use this book, the power of God to unlock, release and receive your baby will be unleashed into your life and home.

Chapter One

The Father's Will and Purpose

Chapter One

The Father's Will and Purpose

"To everything there is a season; a time for every purpose under heaven"

(Ecclesiastes 3:1).

There is a season, and time appointed for your child to be born. God has a purpose for your life and your family. He has a purpose for your child. It is time to rest in Him.

God's intention to preserve His creation is through procreation – blessing of the womb – the first blessing pronounced on humanity, by Him. Who then, can curse whom God has blessed. If you are not already on God's side, then I will advise you to reposition yourself, and be on God's side. Procreation is the only way that God plans for humanity to continue to exist. God cannot contradict Himself. If God should withhold the blessing of the womb from a couple, it must be for a reason and a season. Study through the Bible reveals that when God closes a womb, it is for a reason and a season. Hannah's case is an exemplary one. God knew Israel would need a priest at a specific point in time; therefore, He delayed the coming of Samuel for an appointed time. In another instance, the Lord closed the womb of Rachel in order to release Joseph into His purpose, at an appointed time. In the New Testament, Zechariah and Elizabeth had a prolonged delay for a reason, and a season which was later revealed. John the Baptist, their long awaited son, was in the plan of God – a forerunner to the ministry of our Lord Jesus Christ. He was born six months before Jesus (Luke 1:36). So when the Lord delays the coming of a child, it is usually for His own purpose to be fulfilled.

God, the unchangeable changer, the One who is not the author of confusion, will not contradict Himself. The One in Whom there is no variableness or any shadow of turning, is the One Who is the same yesterday, today and forever. He is the One Whom His Word is Yes and Amen. He lives up to His name. In the days of old, He met needs of couples; in contemporary times He continues to meet couple's needs, of which I and many other families are living testimonies. He would still meet these needs in the future.

There is no lie in the historical account of the Bible as to the fact that God closed the wombs of several women. He is a God of purpose, and He chose to work in the lives of these women for specific purposes. You can also read my book titled *"Joyful Mother of Children."* I am pleased to announce that in due course, God opened the women's wombs. Those women were chosen for specific reasons. The only woman who did not give birth in the Bible was Michal. Her womb was not closed. She did not give birth because David, her husband, refused to meet with her, haven despised him when he danced to the Lord.

Does it now mean that God is playing with peoples' lives and destiny? No, it just shows that God has plans for His creation, and He has the power to do as He pleases.

Whatever the cause of delay is, rest assured that God wants you to be victorious. For He also says in Leviticus 26:9,

> *"For I will look on you favourably and make you fruitful, multiply you and confirm my covenant with you."*

As God has promised, so He will do. You need to prophesy this to yourselves until this becomes a reality in your home because it is the plan of God for you.

Essentially, a foundation of the phrase 'door of the womb' must be laid before I proceed with the main teaching. For a category, the door of the womb has been locked against the babies. To unlock and release something, logic tells me a key or code is required.

This book is not in any way implying all infertility cases are of spiritual origin. My research into the causes of infertility revealed this could be due to several other factors such as health issues like fibroid, hormonal imbalance, stress, and low sperm count. Nevertheless, spiritual issues like, disobedience to God and authority, involvement with the occult, and the devil's oppression cannot be overlooked. And of course, the hand of God, His wisdom and purpose, all play a crucial part in fertility. I will explain myself later in this chapter.

No matter the cause of infertility, there is a higher authority that is able to tackle such problem, and turn situations around. That higher authority is JESUS CHRIST. The mercy of God is available.

"Now Elizabeth's full time came for her to be delivered, and she brought forth a son. When her neighbours and relatives heard how the Lord had shown great mercy to her, they rejoiced with her" (Luke 1:57-58).

Accordingly, the Lord shall show great mercy upon you such that your relatives and neighbours shall rejoice with you.

THE WOMB

There are several scriptures which indicate there are entry doors that protect the womb. These doors can be shut or open. Many of these scriptures tell us certain women could not conceive because their wombs were closed. Job in his affliction actually blamed God for not shutting the doors of his mother's womb.

"Because it did not shut up the doors of my mother's womb" (Job 3:10).

The womb, medically known as uterus, is described by Gray's Anatomy of the human body as a hollow, thick-walled, muscular organ situated deeply in the pelvic cavity between the bladder and rectum. This is where fertilised eggs embed, are housed, and nurtured until full development and delivery.

ANATOMY OF THE UTERUS

The Uterus is also known as the womb. The lower narrow portion of the uterus is called the cervix and it protrudes downward into the opening of the vaginal canal. The vaginal canal extends downward to the external female genitalia (See Figure below). The uterine tubes or Fallopian tubes, on the other hand, extend from either sides of the uterus and act as a channel for eggs from the ovary to travel into the uterus. Sperm travelling from the vagina moves through the cervix into the womb and then into the fallopian tube where fertilisation takes place after which fertilised egg moves back into the womb to be embedded.

Anatomically, the womb has three doorways leading in and out of it, and these three are left uncovered. Physiologically, the fallopian tubes are open at all times for easy ingress and egress. There is an exception with the cervix in the sense that its opening and closure is controlled by the woman's cyclical period. Depending on the stage in the menstrual cycle the secretion protecting the womb thicken up and therefore restricts the access of sperm. At another stage of the cycle, the secretion lightens up to allow easy access of semen. During pregnancy the cervix is designed to remain shut until the very last stages. Opening of the cervix at an earlier stage of pregnancy could result in a miscarriage or premature birth.

That said, under normal circumstance, these doorways should remain patent enough to allow for every stage of reproduction. However, closure may occur due to God's plan, health conditions, demonic oppression or a combination of reasons.

The purpose of doors set in buildings is to control flow and provide protection. I think it would be fair to say the same of the womb. God has purposely set three openings into and out of the womb. Since God pronounced His blessing of fruitfulness and multiplication, the door has been left open as physiologically required. This is the reason why children come even to those who do not deserve them; those who have them unplanned. In infertility, the question must be asked, "Is this happening because of clinical or spiritual reasons, or both?"

As the following scriptures would indicate, God is in control of the opening and closing of the womb.

"When the LORD saw that Leah was unloved,
He opened her womb; *but Rachel was
barren. So Leah conceived and bore a son, and
she called his name Reuben; for she said, "The
LORD has surely looked on my affliction. Now
therefore, my husband will love me"*
(Genesis 29:31-32, Emphasis Mine).

In other words, Leah's womb was shut for a
reason, and she consequently became infertile
for years. However, her breakthrough came after
the Lord opened her womb.

*"Then God remembered Rachel, and God
listened to her and **opened her womb**. And
she conceived and bore a son, and said, "God
has taken away my reproach." So she called his
name Joseph, and said, "The LORD shall add to
me another son"*
(Genesis 30:22-24, Emphasis Mine).

When God remembered Rachel, He listened
to her and opened her womb. She had Joseph.

These scriptures alluded that Leah's and
Rachel's wombs were previously closed. When a
door is closed, nothing can go in or out. As seen
in the anatomical structure of the uterus, the
fallopian tubes are open at all times while the
opening and closing of the cervix is controlled
hormonally just for a number of days every

month. You cannot open what is already opened.

If you also look at the Anatomy of the womb you will find there are three openings leading into and out of the womb. Anatomically, the womb is not closed by any flap, but it could be closed for clinical reasons like blocked or kinked fallopian tubes.

The closure of Hannah's womb was congruent with the purpose of God. God knew that Israel would require a prophet. Consequently, He closed Hannah's womb until His appointed time.

> *"But to Hannah he would give a double portion for he loved Hannah, although the* **Lord had closed her womb***"*
> (1 Samuel 1:5, Emphasis Mine).

It can be deduced from these scriptures, that God is the highest authority Who is in control of the womb. The ultimate power to open the womb belongs to Him particularly where there is demonic interference. The point is; Jesus opened the door over 2000 years ago. The enemy may want you to believe he is the one in charge, but from the scriptures above, God is the one in charge. I would urge you to turn to Him wholeheartedly for help even while seeking medical help. Stop fretting over what you know is out of your control.

Regardless of the cause of the closure, whether it is due to demonic oppression, personal inadequacies, or health issues, a key is required to unlock the door to the womb before the baby can be released and received. There is a process involved. If God has closed the womb, you need to seek His face to understand His purpose and plan, asking for His grace where necessary.

Chapter Two

The Creative Power in the Word of God

Chapter Two

The Creative Power in the Word of God

*M*any years ago, I was confronted with a disease that could have destroyed my liver. It looked as if there was no help for me. I was told by my doctor that the condition would not be treated because it was too late and that I would have to go through the course of the disease. I cried and sought the face of God. During my degree programme, five years after the initial diagnosis, I found out how this illness behaves. So I went into the word of God to find the most appropriate scripture for it. I was glad I found one that was specific to the disease. I began to proclaim the word over my body every day. By the end of one year, I asked my Doctor to investigate the disease again. He explained to me that it could not have disappeared and that I would go through the course of the disease, for life. However, he said, if that was what I wanted, he was willing to do it. So he carried out the investigation again. On the day of my graduation from University, I received the report that the disease had gone. There is an unexplainable power in His word.

> *"In the beginning was the Word, and the Word was with God, and the Word was God. He was in the beginning with God. All things were made through Him, and without Him nothing was made that was made. In Him was life, and the life was the light of men. And the light shines in the darkness, and the darkness did not comprehend it*
>
> (John 1:1-5).

> *"And the Word became flesh and dwelt among us, and we beheld His glory, the glory as of the only begotten of the Father, full of grace and truth"* (John 1:14).

It is this same Word Who was with God in the beginning, Genesis 1:1-10; Who was spoken to the chaos of the face of the deep and from nothing brought about the world. All things were made through Him. What you desire to see in your life could be brought about by and through Him. Do you desire a baby or healing? He is more than able.

God essentially called the world forth by His spoken word. If we are supposed to be of God, then this is one attribute we need to exemplify. We should begin to walk as if we truly are His children. Because our Father is of faith, we cannot begin to act like wimps or faithless children. A young lion cannot begin to act like sheep if it indeed was brought up by his lion parents. As God's children, we need to begin to take authority and dominion through the spoken word. When a king speaks, who would dare to stand up and question his authority?

"Where the word of a king is, there is power; and who may say to him, "What are you doing?" (Ecclesiastes 8:4).

You need to realise and begin to act like you know who you are. Let the lion in you come out. Contrary to what you may have believed, you are not an ugly duckling. You are that beautiful white swan who can fly and soar. You have the power in your hand; all authority has been given to you. Do not let the devil cheat you any further. When you take your stand to authoritatively declare the word of God for your life, then the devil, sickness and even infertility are in trouble. You can call dead reproductive system back to life.

> *"As it is written, 'I have made you a father of many nations' in the presence of Him whom he believed — God, who gives life to the dead **and calls those things which do not exist as though they did"***
>
> (Romans 4:17, Emphasis mine).

This is where you need to start from – knowing where the illness is; where the devil is oppressing you. You then see what God says about the situation. The word of God that applies to your situation needs to be sought after. Finding the word of God that applies to your situation is one of the keys to finding a solution to infertility.

> *"My son, give attention to my words; incline your ear to my sayings. Do not let them depart from your eyes; keep them in the midst of your heart; for they are life to those who find them and health to all their flesh. Keep your heart with all diligence, for out of it spring the issues of life"* (Proverbs 4:20-23).

The scripture above gives directives on how to treat and handle the word. When you have found it, you need to acknowledge it, concentrate on it, be aware of it, give it a thought, consider and register your interest in it. If you have found the word, you have found life and health to all your flesh, including your womb. If the cause of delay is due to health issues like fibroid, blocked fallopian tubes, or endometriosis, know that because you have found the word of God you have found health. That is what the Bible says.

The word of God is not mere word. The word of God is inseparable from His person.

"For your promises are backed by all the honor of your name" (Psalm 138:2b, NLT).

In the biblical culture, it was common for rulers to abuse their authority, violate their own rules and break their promises. But our God is different from earthly and sinful rulers. He exalts His Word by His authority and lives by His own rules. That is just what one would expect from a Just and Loving God, Who lives by His own rules and keeps His promises. One could not have asked for a better God, or a better example.

In this scripture, God is saying, "mention my name whenever you refer to any of my promises, and I am able to defend it as well as back it up." He honours His word. If God honours His word, who are we not to honour His word?

THE VALIDITY OF GOD'S WORD

In research, there are tests called validity and reliability tests. These tests are to determine the authenticity of a research and its findings. If a research should fail on these two tests, then the findings of the research are believed to be unreliable. These tests show that if the research were carried out 100 times or more, the results would be the same. Should there be any difference in these results; the research result would be classed as invalid and unreliable.

Over several Millennia, the reliability and authenticity of the word of God remains indisputable. The word of God has been through much reliability and validity tests, and these have been proven sure, time and again. As scientists tried to disprove its reliability, more evidence to support it came to light. They began to wonder why they ventured into researching the authenticity of God's word. However, it was too late.

Medical knowledge has also tried to disprove the genuineness of God's word. However, this has amazingly discovered that its foundation is deeply seated in God Himself. Archaeological evidence could only find evidence to support the validity of God's word.

History has it that the Bible was written by 40 authors, over 1600 years, covering 60 generations, from different backgrounds. It is amazingly and awesomely noteworthy that the Bible never lost its message throughout this period. The beauty of agreement and continuity is clearly demonstrated. The word of God has been proven by Christian researchers and archaeological evidences, through the testimonies of people who have encountered the power of God.

In spite of the many storms and criticisms suffered by the scripture (from tearing to burning), it has been miraculously preserved in history, for generations past, present and future. I think this is commendable! However, the sad story is that many carry the word and only see it as some words written in black and white and perhaps a few red letters, bonded with genuine leather or fashionable covering. I am not surprised it is not working for some.

In the next few chapters, I will be exploring the power in the word of God; how your spirit can be lifted up through the word; and how to release and activate the power in the word.

Maybe you have questioned God's hand in the Bible, debating it was written by mere men. I want to ask you to have a rethink as these men were inspired by the Holy Spirit to write the scripture (2 Peter 1:19-21).

The Bible is the handwriting of God which can never be erased by anything – man, situations or circumstances. In fact, the more you try to erase, the bolder it becomes. I want to challenge you to take the word and use it to redress situations that are confronting you. You have argued against the word enough. Arguing cannot and has never changed anything about the Bible. Argue for the Bible and you will be amazed, dazed, and dazzled at the change that the word can bring into your life and situation. Your words cannot change the word of God but the Word of God can change your words, life and situation. May be your word has always been, 'I cannot bear children' but the word of God can change your words to 'I am now a joyful mother of children.'

Chapter Three

He stands to see His Word Fulfilled

Chapter Three

He stands to see His Word Fulfilled

"For the rain comes down and snow from heaven and do not return there, but water the earth and make it bring forth and bud, that it may give seed to the sower and bread to the eater. So shall my word be that goes out from my mouth; it shall not return to me void but it shall accomplish what I please and it shall prosper in the thing for which I sent it" (Isaiah 55:10-11).

God likens his word to rain and snow, over which no-one has control. As human beings, we do not have the power to turn them on and fill the earth, cover the ground, water the earth, and make it evaporate back to the heavens in the same form they came. So far, I have not come across any account of such. In the scripture above, God declared His plan through His spoken word:

> ➢ To water the earth,
> ➢ To bring about fruitfulness (bring forth and bud),
> ➢ To give seed to the sower and bread to the eater

"Unless the LORD builds the house, they labor in vain who build it; unless the LORD guards the city, the watchman stays awake in vain. It is vain for you to rise up early, to sit up late, to eat the bread of sorrows; for so He gives His beloved sleep" (Psalm 127:1-2).

Human effort alone does not guarantee fruitfulness. Our desires and needs can only be met in God. Many lives are dry and unfruitful because they are not watered by God. Without rain, farmers will tell you their crops do not stand a good chance of surviving. God puts His seal of approval on His word by saying that His word will not return to Him void, but it shall accomplish what He has purposed it to do and prosper in the things for which He has sent it. The English Standard Version states, *"it shall not return to Me empty."* That is to say; it shall not return to God without fruit.

When God speaks, it must bear fruit. God does not speak empty or vague words. His words have a mission to accomplish. God already spoke your baby. He said, *"None shall be barren in the land."* He does not expect that word to return to Him without accomplishing the purpose in your life. It is left for you to take the word and apply it to your situation. It is time to stop worrying yourself about the magnitude of your problem; stop wondering how one verse of scripture could undo what the enemy did.

God's word will not accomplish halfway, almost or very close to His intended purpose, but it will yield full result. In His word, there is nothing like, "it almost happened." All of God's word has its own purpose. God's assurance on this is very certain. Failure to see the manifestation of God's word in your life is not God's fault.

For every situation that confronts you in life, God has already spoken into that situation. It is your responsibility, however, to search such words out, begin to declare them, and affirm them in your situation.

> *"It is the glory of God to conceal a matter, but the glory of kings is to search out a matter'* (Proverbs 25:2).

Every child of God is a king, and it is your glory to search out what He declared about your entitlement before the beginning of time.

God said that His word is forever settled in heaven. Thank God because His word is forever settled in heaven, not on earth, not in the house of Parliament but settled in heaven. Your enemies do not have access or power to unsettle it. Any doubt you may have does not have sufficient power to change what God has already declared. Forever means, it is eternally, everlastingly, perpetually, ceaselessly, evermore settled. It is reassuring to know that His word is eternally constant.

"And the scripture cannot be broken"
(John 10:35).

The scripture is God's law, and just as statutory or the common law of a nation cannot be trampled upon, also the scripture cannot be trampled or broken. People may break human law, and somehow get away with it; the scripture cannot be broken. Even the devil knows the scripture cannot be broken, although he uses his scam to scare people into believing the scripture has been broken. How is it that I am not getting pregnant if the scripture cannot be broken? In most cases, the devil has pulled the wool over many people's eyes thereby resulting in ignorance. Sadly, many believers do not know the authority they have in Jesus Christ or His word. The devil is cheating those who do not know their right.

> *"'I have given you authority to trample on snakes and scorpions and to overcome all the powers of the enemies and nothing shall by any means hurt you'"* (Luke 10:19).

God assured Jeremiah in Jeremiah 1:12,

"I am ready to perform my word"

This word of assurance also comes to you today. God is ready to perform His word. The axe is already laid at the root of the tree of barrenness. The point is that:

> *"God is not a man that He should lie, nor a son of man that He should repent, has He said, will He not do? Or has He spoken, and will He not make it good? God is not an author of confusion"* (Numbers 23:19).

He stands by His word. Since no one can challenge His ways, knowledge, work or promises, He will not lie to you about anything. After all, no one has ever punished His judgements, deeds or acts. Therefore, I stand up to affirm that the testimony of My Lord, King,

Friend and Master stands sure with this inscription,

"For all the promises of God in Him are Yes, and in Him Amen, to the glory of God through us" (2 Corinthians 1:20).

On this note, I will admonish you to resolve in your heart that God's word is sure. God will help you as you do so.

LIFE IN THE WORD

The word of God is ubiquitous. It is like a messenger sent to deliver a message. His word does not only travel, but it also moves faster than you could ever imagine.

"He sends out His commands to the earth; His word runs swiftly" (Psalm 147:15).

"He sent His word and healed them, and delivered them from their destructions" (Psalm 107:20).

There is more to God's word than one could ever think or imagine.

"For the word of God is living and powerful, and sharper than any two-edged sword, piercing even to the division of soul and spirit,

and of joints and marrow, and is a discerner of the thoughts and intents of the heart" (Hebrews 4:12).

Once the word is sent to a situation, the Bible tells us the word begins to work in the situation. As depicted in the scripture above, the word of God has the following qualities:

Living

Let us take a look at the qualities of living things around us. They exhibit the signs of life. When something has life, it means it can grow, move and probably bring forth fruit. Now consider the word of God being the life is capable of movement. If the word of God is living that means it has life, it is alive. This quality is further confirmed as below:

"It is the Spirit who gives life; the flesh profits nothing. The words that I speak to you are spirit, and they are life" (John 6:63).

Medicines and many substances have shelf lives and subsequently will expire. However, the word of God cannot expire because it is the life. It is eternally preserved.

This is the reason why God was able to swear by Himself to Abraham. So He can show the immutability of His counsel, God confirmed His word with an oath (Hebrews 6:13-18). Whatever has life can breathe. May the word of God breathe life to every dead organ in your body and situation.

Powerful

The word of God is loaded with 'Dunamis' – the dynamic power of God. The power in the word will shatter into pieces every chain of infertility and miscarriage.

The gospel of John describes the Word of God as Jesus Christ. I will share more about the name in a later chapter.

Sharper than any two edged sword

The word of God is sharper than what you consider sharp and is able to cut through the toughest situation. The word is a two edged sword; it is not one sided. This tells me something. It has a greater impact when used appropriately. Whatever two-edged sword cuts through can never be put together again. I prophesy that, as that double edged sword is laid at the root of that barrenness, it will cut asunder every associated problem, as well. It can never be mended or put together again by the enemy.

Piercing even to the division of the soul and spirit, and of joints and marrow

The word does not only take care of the physical, but it goes deeper into the soul and the spirit. What are the seeds that have been sown into the seat of your emotions? Is your spirit telling you it can never happen for you? Do you think that evil spirits are at work in your situation? I have come to tell you that the word of God can pierce through such. No evil spirit is so tough that cannot be pierced by the word of God. Maybe you have been told the spiritual husband or the soul mate has so much bound itself to your spirit and soul, that there is nothing else that can be done. There is good news – the word of God can pierce through.

> *"He who sins is of the devil, for the devil has sinned from the beginning. For this purpose the Son of God was manifested, that He might destroy the works of the devil"* (1 John 3:8).

Discerner of the thoughts and intents of the heart

His word is a discerner of the thoughts and intents of the heart. It tells us *"The heart is deceitful above all things, and desperately wicked; who can know it?"* No one, but the word of God can discern our thoughts and intents of the heart. So the word of God can get to where a Doctor, Pastor, Medicine or surgery cannot reach.

In light of these, I implore you, by the mercies of God, to let the word of God work in your situation. Many of us are fond of talking about our situations. When we go to see the Doctor, they ask us to talk about the situation. When my patients come to see me, I ask them to tell me about their condition in order to get an understanding of what the problem is and the likely solution. We talk about the problem to our friends and whoever wishes to listen. I also found that I talk about my problem to God. But God is not asking us to talk to Him about the problem. Just as He instructed Ezekiel at the valley of the dry bones, He is telling you to speak to the problem.

"And He said to me, 'Son of man, can these bones live? So I answered O Lord God, You know" (Ezekiel 37::3).

Rick Joyner in his book titled, The Final Quest, quoted his friend's statement, 'When the Omniscient God asks you a question, it is not because He is seeking information.'

This statement applies to Ezekiel in the valley of dry bones. God already has the answer although He wanted to stir something up in

Ezekiel. Knowing God, Ezekiel also decided to sit on the fence. He refused to answer a 'yes' or 'no.' If he were not a man of faith and wisdom, he could have gone into dialogue with God over this issue. He would have said something like 'God, Abba; you can see how dry these bones are. Very dry and they are many. You would not even know which one is leg bone or arm bone. Forget about these bones God.' He knew God has the answer to the question. So he replied Him, 'O Lord God, you know.' Now look at what God said following Ezekiel's reply,

> *"Again He said, 'prophesy to these bones, hear the word of the Lord!"* (Ezekiel 37:4).

God did not say, 'speak about these bones, how many are they, how dry are they, how few are they, how long or short are they?' He said, *'prophesy to these bones, hear the word of the Lord.'* Prophesy the word of God to that situation regardless of what its nature is; how long you've had it; how bad or chronic it seems; how irreparable the condition is, and regardless of how dead your condition may appear. Say to it, *"hear the word of the Lord."* These situations have ears, and they can hear and obey the word of the Lord.

Say what you desire to see; not what the enemy is taunting you with. Not what the condition is telling you or what you have been told by a doctor will be the normal course for your condition.

Thus says the Lord God to you 'womb': 'surely I will cause the baby to embed and live in you for nine months, and this baby shall be delivered and live.' If this is what you want to see, then prophesy it. Prophecies are not mere words. They are words of encouragement; saying what you desire to see in the future. It is like you have already seen into the future and declaring what the future will be in the now. You need to see it happening, with the eyes of faith, though a new result may be telling you otherwise. We are called believers because our walk with Him is not a walk by sight but by faith. It is not an ordinary walk but an extraordinary and supernatural walk.

> "Seeing then that we have a great High Priest who has passed through the heavens, Jesus the Son of God, let us hold fast our confession. For we do not have a High Priest who cannot sympathize with our weaknesses, but was in all points tempted as we are, yet without sin. Let us therefore come boldly to the throne of grace, that we may obtain mercy and find grace to help in time of need"
>
> (Hebrews 4:14-16).

Let us hold fast our confession. What is your confession? Are you saying what God is saying or what your situation is saying? For we have a great high priest who has passed through the heavens, touched by what we are going through and can sympathise with us. Not like the high priest of the Old Testament, Jesus was tested at every point. No, He has never suffered any physical miscarriages and has never had to wait for the fruit of the womb but has suffered a miscarriage of justice when he was chosen to be killed in place of Barabbas. He has had to wait for you to turn your heart to Him, and He is still waiting for many out there.

Can you imagine waiting to receive what is normally yours? Can you imagine the pain He went through just for us? Can you put a price or measure on the suffering He went through? Can you imagine His torn skin from several whiplashes He received? Can you quantify how many pints of blood He lost? Can you begin to imagine the shame He went through? He was able to raise the dead and open blinded eyes, yet He died such a horrific death. He has been through it too and so can sympathise with you.

I challenge you to think about it. You therefore need to be tenacious in holding on the word of His promise. In all of these things He suffered, the Bible tells us we are more than conquerors through Him. Is this not an amazing mystery? He secured victory, healing, deliverance, salvation for us on the cross.

Your Confession

Prayer - Lord I choose to walk with You because whoever walks with You does not have anything to fear and worry about. Thank You Jesus because I know You are on the lead, and I follow after You steadfastly. I hold tight unto You and Your unfailing love. I put my whole trust in You.

Chapter Four

The Place of Faith in
Confessing the Word of God

Chapter Four

The Place of Faith in Confessing the Word of God

𝒯his chapter aims to awaken faith even in hopeless cases. God's perspective on faith will be explored with the intention of taking us to a higher dimension of faith. What is Faith and how can someone be sure they are walking in true faith and not presumption?

WHAT IS FAITH?

Strong's concordance and dictionary defines faith from the Greek word 'Pistis' meaning conviction, trust, belief, reliance, trustworthiness and persuasion. It is the divinely implanted principle of inward confidence, assurance, trust, and reliance in God and all that He says.

Hebrews 11:1 defines faith as,

"The substance of things hoped for, the evidence of things not seen".

From the faith definitions above, it is obvious faith has two elements: substance and evidence. In order to be able to present evidence to a court of law, you need to be able to substantiate your evidence. Substance is something you can hold on to, gist, matter, and stuff. It is the substance; stuff you have to hold on to when all else is stripped away. It is the source of one's strength, something that keeps you going. It is your clarity that you have what you believe for. The woman with the issue of blood said 'if only I can touch the hem of His garment, that is, if only I can take hold of that substance, I know I shall be made whole.'

What is that assurance you could lay your spiritual finger on that other people may not be able to substantiate? If only you can lay hold to that word that you need and allow it to sink into your spirit. The disciples did query Jesus when He insisted someone touched Him. The woman touched Jesus' garment, the substance, yet those around her took no notice. However, Jesus felt it.

The substance aspect of faith has to do with what transpires between you and King Jesus, the anointed one.

Evidence, on the other hand, is something to show others when you are asked for a proof. It is something to show your accusers, adversary, confronters, and mockers. It is the report of your investigation. How can you show or present something that is not yet visible? Without a tangible substance, there cannot be tangible evidence. The word of God is the evidence. If you venture into presenting any other evidence when you are being questioned, you do not stand any chance of withstanding the drill of the accuser. When reminded you can no longer have a baby and that you have reached menopause or illness would not allow pregnancy, produce the word of God as your evidence. Tell them it is written:

> *"Behold, children are a heritage from the* LORD, *the fruit of the womb is a reward"* (Psalm 127:3).

> *"No one shall suffer miscarriage or be barren in your land; I will fulfill the number of your days"* (Exodus 23:26).

Say it to yourself several times: 'I have the heritage of the Lord, and I shall not be barren in the land according to the word of His power.'

And so the devil, usually disguised in human clothing keeps quiet or finds someone else to taunt. I waited for the fruit of the womb for four years. My doctor reminded me on several occasions that I was not meant to have any children even when I missed my period. On one of the occasions I had to stand up to him, to declare what the word of God says.

I held on to the word of God that says 'the things which are seen are made from the things that are not seen.' Conception is a mystery. No one has ever discerned the actual time fertilization takes place. Conception is a holy or private issue. Have you ever seen your egg as it is released from your ovaries? Have you ever seen with your bare eyes your husband's sperm swimming in semen on the bed perhaps? The doctor was walking by sight but I was walking by faith.

Again, Hebrews 11:1 says, *"Now faith is ..."* Faith is a now thing; not a yesterday thing. It is not something to practice today, abandon for the next few weeks, and then again pick up somewhere along the line. You have to be consistent in your faith walk. You cannot confess positive this minute, and the next minute curse yourself and expect faith to work for you.

Let me therefore paraphrase Hebrews 11:1 as follows:

"Now faith is something you have to convince yourself and show others that what you are expecting God to do in your life will surely manifest" (My definition of faith based on Hebrews 11:1).

MIX IT WITH FAITH

I would liken faith to a two-way cord that connects you to God and God to you. Through one cord you are able to connect and receive from God and through the other, God can reach out to you and deliver to you. Without faith, you cannot reach Him and He cannot reach you. Romans 5:2 tells us that we have access to His grace by faith. Whatever you are trusting God for, you will only receive through grace, and you cannot have access to His grace except by faith. Jesus tells us,

*"Because of your unbelief; for assuredly, I say to you, if you have faith as a **mustard seed**, you will say to this mountain, 'Move from here to there,' and it will move; and nothing will be impossible for you"* (Matthew 17:20, Emphasis mine).

A friend of mine who recently returned from Holy Land trip brought me a cluster of mustard seeds, and when I looked at it, this verse of scripture became more illuminated. Mustard seed is a seed you could easily miss without knowing – as tiny as dust. In other words, God is not asking for a huge faith to move mountains or huge problems. Imagine such a tiny level of faith, moving a normally immovable mountain. By faith, Abraham pleased God and the men of old received a good report.

It was by faith that even Sarah was able to have a child, though she was barren and was too old. She believed that God would keep his promise (Hebrews 11:11, NLT). God still keeps promises today.

> *"For we also have had the gospel preached to us, just as they did; but the message they heard was of no value to them, because those who heard did not combine it with faith. Now we who have believed enter that rest, just as God has said, so I declared on oath in my anger, 'they shall never enter my rest'"*
>
> (Hebrews 4:2-3, NIV).

The NKJV states the word did not profit them because it did not mix with faith in their hearts. The message preached to the Israelites in the wilderness did not profit them because it was not mixed with faith in their hearts, so God swore they would not enter His rest. For the word of God to profit or benefit us, we need to add an ingredient called 'Faith.' My prayer for you is that, as you have read this word, it will mix with faith in your heart. This word shall profit you, and you shall find rest on every side.

Chapter Five

Thanksgiving

Chapter Five

Thanksgiving

NINA'S STORY

A bungalow sitting alone on a large parcel of land has a precious baby locked away by a strong man. Nina's plan was to enter the huge property to retrieve and release the baby into her welcoming arms. At the same time, Nina was worried about what would happen to her if the strong man should get hold of her while trying to unlock and release the baby. After all, the bible says, *"In fact, no one can enter a strong man's house without first tying him up. Then he can plunder the strong man's house"* (Mark 3:27 NIV).

In her hand was a great big container which was handed to her by her dad. It is called the tub of the great manual. Inside the tub were treasures of instructions for the journey she was to embark upon. Unknown to Nina, the tub could only be as big as the holder perceived it to be. Although she followed an instruction in the manual to find her way to the bungalow, Nina did not give too much attention to the rest of the tub. Rather, she focused her attention on obtaining the master key that would grant access to the building. This seemed to be the right thing to do.

Nina stood close to the main entrance to the building, feeling extremely nervous, and gazing with anxiety from side to side and sweaty, not knowing where to turn or what to do. Her feelings were torn between the success in locating the premises described in the great manual and the daunting consideration of possible problems in being able to gain access to the building. Nina's legs felt wobbly, and one could almost hear her heart pounding nervously. She thought aloud, "I found the directions on how to get to this building in the tub of the great manual. I might as well dig my hands into it again to check if the keys are in here." She began to feel through the tub for the keys as instructed in the great manual. It was like trying to look for a golden ball in a concealed compartment covered with different types of colours. "I have just touched a metal type object," she said with excitement. Nina therefore tucked in with both hands trying to feel for the keys only to find the metal was the plate of a clashing cymbal. Nina brought out a clashing cymbal. You could feel the pulsating disappointment looking at her and at the same time hear the frustration in the tone of her voice as she expressed, "what am I meant to do with a clashing cymbal for goodness sake? Am I meant to hit it against the door or something?" So she dropped the cymbal on the floor in frustration and anger.

She thought having another look through the tub could turn out successful, so Nina again tucked both hands into the tub, moving her hands towards the middle of the treasure box. Nina felt she touched the key on this occasion. With both her sweaty hands still in the tub, she clutched the metal she had found, while struggling to bring it out. She found it was not what anyone would call the master key. It was a trumpet. Frustrated, Nina began to moan. "Who on earth would put such a thing in the tub of the great manual? Can I ever trust the tub to offer and give me what I am looking for? My Father gave me this tub, and he told me that everything I would ever need is inside. How could dad have done this to me? Are his servants who packaged this tub playing some pranks on me? If this is the case, I must report them to Dad."

Nina reached for her mobile phone and rang Dad but the phone kept giving an engaged tone. By this time, Nina was fuming with anger. She mused, "But Dad said that this is His direct line, and told me I would be able to reach Him in one dial. Why am I not able to get through?" On the other end of the phone, the following message kept coming through to Nina, "The person you are calling is unable to answer your call, please hang up and dial again using this code: "P-S-A-L-M-1-0-0:4." Nina was very desperate to talk to her Dad. She would do anything to get through. As she began to redial, Nina began to sing as follow:

"Enter into His gates with thanksgiving, and into His courts with praise. Be thankful to Him, and bless His name, for the LORD *is good; His mercy is everlasting, and His truth endures to all generations"* (Psalm 100:4-5).

Nina did not stop there. She began to praise Him on the trumpet, the Psaltery and Harp as instructed in the great manual, the Bible. She realised what the cymbal she brought out from the tub were for – to praise His name. She made her way towards the door as she continued singing. Then the doors began to open accordingly. Before she knew it, she had already reached the baby. She heaved a huge sigh of relief as she touched and held the baby in her hands. She was glad that the baby she longed for was safe and unharmed.

Praise will open every door that has been shut against you. Praise will connect you to the King of kings and the Lord of lords. Do not stop praising, even when you feel frustrated. A songwriter wrote, 'overcoming every problem begins with a thankful heart.'

I want you to be aware of the three invaluable aspects in thanking God. Firstly, a good understanding of the biblical meaning of thanksgiving is essential when praising God. Secondly, the reasons why God should be praised or thanked even when things are not going well will be examined. Thirdly, I will explore the significance of praise. Lastly, I will also examine a number of biblical examples with particular attention given to the lessons inferred.

Essentially, understanding the root of the word 'thanksgiving,' both from Hebrew and Greek perspectives will enhance understanding of the topic.

WHAT IS THANKSGIVING?

The word 'thanksgiving' is from the Hebrew word 'Todah' meaning thanks, thanksgiving, praise, adoration. Todah is derived from the verb 'Yadah' meaning to give thanks, and the root of Yadah is 'yah' meaning hand (Spirit-filled life bible). This explains the reason why hands are lifted up when praising God.

To thank or praise is to lift or extend one's hands to God in appreciation. Think of meeting and greeting others; a warm handshake signifies thanks and gratefulness. From this point, I will use the words, 'thanksgiving and praise' interchangeably.

WHY SHOULD YOU PRAISE GOD?

It is a command and God's will

"In everything give thanks; for this is the will of God in Christ Jesus for you"
(1 Thessalonians 5:18).

If you desire to obey God's commands, start praising Him. If you are yearning to do His will, praise Him. With praising God, you cannot go wrong.

"Offer unto God thanksgiving, and pay your vows to the Most High" (Psalm 50:14).

To offer something means to present something to someone, and there is a possibility for it to be considered, accepted, or rejected. David knew this and he said,

"Let the words of my mouth and the meditation of my heart be acceptable in Your sight, O LORD, my strength and my Redeemer" (Psalm 19:14).

In view of this, it is not in our place to withhold praise from God based on one's feelings. You might be going through overwhelming challenges, yet I will encourage you to praise Him.

"For our present troubles are small and won't last very long. Yet they produce for us a glory that vastly outweighs them and will last forever!" (2 Corinthians 4:17 NLT).

It is a sacrifice and the fruit of your lips

David realised praise is a sacrifice and said,

"Nor will I offer burnt offerings to the LORD my God with that which costs me nothing"
(2 Samuel 24:24).

"So David bought the threshing floor and the oxen for fifty shekels of silver. And David built there an altar to the Lord, and offered burnt offerings and peace offerings. So the Lord heeded the prayers for the land, and the plague

was withdrawn from Israel" (Read the full account in 2 Samuel 24:18-25).

"Take words with you, and return to the LORD. Say to Him, 'Take away all iniquity; receive us graciously, for we will offer the sacrifices of our lips'" (Hosea 14:2).

Praise is not praise until it is verbalized. You must take words with you every time you appear before Him in praise.

"Therefore by Him let us continually offer the sacrifice of praise to God, that is, the fruit of our lips, giving thanks to His name" (Hebrews 13:15).

You may be praising and thanking Him through your tears, emotional pain, or physical pain; these will not go in vain. As God heeded David's prayer because of the sacrifice and withdrew the plague from Israel, the Lord will hear your prayers and withdraw barrenness from your life.

The significance of lifting one's hands in praise

"And the cherubim shall stretch out their wings above, covering the mercy seat with their wings, and they shall face one another;

the faces of the cherubim shall be toward the mercy seat. You shall put the mercy seat on top of the ark, and in the ark you shall put the Testimony that I will give you. And there I will meet with you, and I will speak with you from above the mercy seat, from between the two cherubim which are on the ark of the Testimony, about everything which I will give you in commandment to the children of Israel" (Exodus 25:20-22).

The word 'Cherubim' is from the Hebrew word Keruvim and it is pronounced as (Kehroo-veem). It is the plural of Keruv. They are angelic beings associated with guarding and bearing God's throne. They are associated with the worship of the Lord God Almighty. In fact, according to Strong concordance and Vine's expository dictionary, Keruv may be related to bless, praise, adore.

Furthermore, the wings of the Cherubim spread out, and the Lord said that, He will meet with us and speak with us 'there;' between the outstretched arms. The Cherubs posture is symbolic of how we worship God.

A sister called me on a Sunday morning having been told she has an ectopic pregnancy (when a fetus embeds in a place other than the womb, usually the fallopian tube). This is a potentially fatal condition. God said to me, 'tell her to praise me.' I thought God had missed the point. If nothing is done urgently the woman could bleed to death. However, I still told her to praise God before her hospital appointment later that day, and she did as instructed. When she went back to the hospital she had another scan, and the report showed that the baby had moved into the womb. I realised that God did not miss the point. I did. Today, she has two big boys.

You might think you should have moved beyond the level you currently are. Praise Him regardless of your present situation and He will meet with you and speak to you between your outstretched hands.

Chapter Six

Thank You Sir!

Chapter Six

Thank You, Sir!

While shaking hands with her boss, with tear-filled eyes, Lola expressed, "thank you, sir." Her boss paused for a while before saying a word. "Lola, I have just informed you that your job is also on the line; are you thanking me for this?" replied Andrew. He continued, "Your invaluable contribution to this company over the past five years is appreciated. However, there is an urgent need necessitating that at least 500 employees be laid off if this company is to survive this hard time. Sorry, I cannot guarantee anything." Lola replied, "Sir, I am thankful for the opportunity to work with you and for believing in me these five years. Thank you for the wonderful career path as well as the time you took in explaining the company's new plan on a one-to-one basis. Without this job, things will not be the same at home. Nevertheless, I am still grateful." Lola left Andrew's office sobbing quietly.

Andrew became very restless after Lola left his office. "I have got to find a way of protecting this girl's job," he exclaimed! Andrew paced up and down in his office with his right hand slightly grabbing his chin for a few minutes. However, he concluded it was a hopeless case.

A couple of months later, Andrew received a telephone call. As he picked the call, he recognised the voice at the other end. This is an unusual call, he thought. "Good afternoon sir," he said, and then paused while rummaging through the pieces of paper on his desk. He quickly reached out for his pen, and began to scribble on a scuffled piece of paper. Then he responded, "Lola Smith," and paused again. "Yes, I am sure, thank you, sir," Andrew replied, as he hung up the phone. "Yes! Yes!" he exclaimed. His countenance changed.

What happened to Andrew? Who was the caller on the other end and what information was passed across to him over the phone? Surprisingly, the company's CEO had called from the head office to inform Andrew that the company has decided to retain one post from each of the 10 branches affected by the job cut.

Andrew had been asked to nominate a staff he would like to retain. Obviously, Andrew nominated Lola.

Overcoming every problem begins with a thankful heart. If you are thankful, your tank will be full. This is just a biblical principle. I am not asking you to thank God so that you can have what you want or desire. Rather my aim is to help you to see what God desires of you, even in the hard times, and this in turn will be the more reasons for which to be more thankful.

Let us explore further. What does it mean to complain? We will examine the implications of an unthankful heart and share biblical insights that exemplify gratitude.

THE VOICE OF COMPLAINING

The Oxford English Dictionary defines 'complain' as "to express dissatisfaction or annoyance."

It is normal to be dissatisfied or express dissatisfaction about unpleasant issues one is experiencing. However, care must be taken to ensure that it does not amount to complaining or murmuring, especially against God. We must learn not to complain against God, and the people he has set over us. When we complain against God's servant, we are complaining against God (Exodus 17:1-4).

Apostle Paul admonished that requests should be made known to God with prayers and supplications with thanksgiving.

"Be anxious for nothing, but in everything by prayer and supplication, with thanksgiving, let your requests be made known to God; and the peace of God, which surpasses all understanding, will guard your hearts and minds through Christ Jesus"

(Philippians 4:6-7).

"The voice of joy and the voice of gladness, the voice of the bridegroom and the voice of the bride, the voice of those who will say: 'Praise the Lord of hosts, For the Lord is good, for His mercy endures forever' — and of those who will bring the sacrifice of praise into the house of the Lord. For I will cause the captives of the land to return as at the first,' says the Lord"
(Jeremiah 33:11).

This scripture alludes that there are many voices that can be raised to God. The Psalmist knew this and said,

"That I may proclaim with the voice of thanksgiving, and tell of all Your wondrous works" (Psalm 26:7).

What voice are you lifting up to God; the voice of thanksgiving or complaint? The other side of thanksgiving is complaining.

The amazing thing is that; God can hear whatever voice you lift up to Him, therefore, raise a voice of thanksgiving in every situation. I know it can be very challenging, especially if you believe you are doing all the right things to satisfy God whereas those that are not, are getting the blessing you desire. Complaint is displeasing to God and it attracts His fury.

> *"And in the morning you shall see the glory of the LORD; for He hears your complaints against the LORD. But what are we that you complain against us? And the LORD spoke to Moses, saying, 'I have heard the complaints of the children of Israel. Speak to them, saying, 'At twilight you shall eat meat, and in the morning you shall be filled with bread. And you shall know that I am the LORD your God'''* (Exodus 16:7, 11-12).

> *"Now when the people complained, it displeased the LORD; for the LORD heard it, and His anger was aroused. So the fire of the LORD burned among them, and consumed some in the outskirts of the camp"*
> (Numbers 11:1).

God can hear us when we complain. This can arouse His anger as it did among the Israelites such that God's fire broke out in fury until Moses interceded for them. One would have thought that they had learnt their lesson but surprisingly, they did not (Numbers 11:4-6). Their weeping and complaining carried on such that God's fury arose again, and Moses also was displeased (Numbers 11:10). Who would intercede for them on this occasion? God became annoyed with their complaints such that He gave them more than they could handle but not enjoy (Numbers 11:18-20).

"But while the meat was still between their teeth, before it was chewed, the wrath of the LORD was aroused against the people, and the LORD struck the people with a very great plague" (Numbers 11:33).

If complaining against the Lord is normal for you, I admonish you to repent today and ask the Lord to always help you to look for a reason to praise and thank Him. Complaining attracts the wrath of God on your life. Read the full account in Numbers 11:1-34.

THANK HIM, NOW!

Recently, I watched a Christian documentary on TV. It was about a mother of four children who have been crippled for decades. She had always crawled on all fours to get from point A to B in order to go about her normal daily activities. She was visited by a Charity organisation who donated a wheelchair to her. The bright smile on her face and that of her family brought tears to my eyes. And I thought, "but she is still crippled, yet the joy that flooded her heart with the donation of a wheelchair was noteworthy." I felt challenged by her heart of gratitude. God loves a heart of gratitude. Thank Him Now, SELAH!

BENEFITS OF THANKSGIVING

Praise will help you through your pain and midnight season

Paul and Silas decided to praise God in the prison after they had been beaten because of their zeal for Jesus.

> *"But at midnight Paul and Silas were praying and singing hymns to God, and the prisoners were listening to them"* (Acts 16:25).

Midnight signifies the most difficult period of a challenge – a time where there is nowhere else to turn. It is a difficult place to be. It is a time when one feels abandoned by the people who are meant to help. Friends, pastor, family, in-laws, and medical personnel, may turn their backs. It is a period of vulnerability and loneliness; when everywhere is dark, and you cannot even make a decision. The Bible records that, at this point, Paul and Silas decided that they would not be moved by their situation but instead offer the SACRIFICE of praise to God. In fact, midnight is a perfect time to give praises to Him.

"At midnight I will rise to give thanks to You, because of Your righteous judgments"
(Psalm 119:62).

Praise becomes a sacrifice in the midnight of one's circumstance. Read the full account about Paul and Silas in Act 16: 16-33.

Praise will open the prison doors and bring about divine encounter

In the midnight hour, while they were praising God, something unexpected and extraordinary happened.

"Suddenly there was a great earthquake, so that the foundations of the prison were shaken; and immediately all the doors were opened and everyone's chains were loosed. And the keeper of the prison, awaking from sleep and seeing the prison doors open, supposing the prisoners had fled, drew his sword and was about to kill himself. But Paul called with a loud voice, saying, 'Do yourself no harm, for we are all here.' Then he called for a light, ran in, and fell down trembling before Paul and Silas. And he brought them out and said, 'Sirs, what must I do to be saved?'" (Acts 16:26-30).

An earthquake is an unexpected and undesirable shaking of everything to its foundation. During this shaking, you might be led to believe that your situation has gone from bad to worse. Don't despair! The power of the Almighty God will shake your troubles to its root, and He will bring about your deliverance. The doors of your womb shall be flung open and every chain of oppression shall be loosed.

Praise will bring about deliverance

"Shall the prey be taken from the mighty, or the captives of the righteous be delivered? But thus says the LORD: *'Even the captives of the mighty shall be taken away, and the prey of the terrible be delivered;*

for I will contend with him who contends with you, and I will save your children" (Isaiah 49:24-25).

Praise will bring joy and peace to your heart

"Sing praise to the LORD, you saints of His, and give thanks at the remembrance of His holy name. For His anger is but for a moment, His favour is for life; weeping may endure for a night, but joy comes in the morning" (Psalm 30:4-5).

"You have turned for me my mourning into dancing; You have put off my sackcloth and clothed me with gladness, to the end that my glory may sing praise to You and not be silent. O LORD my God, I will give thanks to You forever" (Psalm 30:11-12).

This is the blessedness of answered prayer.

Praise will cause you to possess the gates of the enemy

The story of Jericho

"So the people shouted when the priests blew the trumpets. And it happened when the

people heard the sound of the trumpet, and the people shouted with a great shout, that the wall fell down flat. Then the people went up into the city, every man straight before him, and they took the city" (Joshua 6:20).

Chapter Seven

Power in Jesus' Name

Chapter Seven

Power in Jesus' Name

THE PERSON OF JESUS CHRIST

Jesus Christ was given a name based on His purpose on earth. In order to have a good grasp of the power in the name, you must have a good understanding of who the person is. Names command authority and respect depending on who the person or individual is, and their influence or the position they occupy in the society.

For instance, if you received a letter from Bill Gates with his signature, offering you a huge amount of money, i.e. £1m, for a particular project, will you be worried that he might not be able to sustain the promise? However, if your colleague at work, who earns just about £700 per month makes the same offer, will you take it seriously?

Biblically and essentially, a name conveys the purpose of God for that individual.

A name must be associated with the person bearing it; they must not be looked at independently.

WHO IS JESUS CHRIST? (John 1:1-16)

There was a dialogue between Jesus and His disciples recorded in Matthew 16:13-20. Jesus asked His disciples about the public opinion of His being. The response was startling as He was presumed to be John the Baptist, Elijah, even Jeremiah or just one of the Prophets. Obviously, people had various perceptions of the person of Jesus. He then questioned His disciples about their own understanding or knowledge of Him?

"He said to them, 'but who do you say that I am?'" (Matthew 16:15).

There are various understanding of the person of Jesus Christ that are not necessarily right. However, as a Christian, it is essential to know who He is in order to get the best out of one's relationship with Him. It is impossible to know Jesus in a physical sense. It is the Holy

Spirit who can convey and give a true revelation of who He is.

> *"Simon Peter answered and said, 'You are the Christ, the Son of the living God.' Jesus answered and said to him, 'Blessed are you, Simon Bar-Jonah, for flesh and blood has not revealed this to you, but My Father who is in heaven'"* (Matthew 16:16-17).

Jesus is still asking the same question today, "but who do you say that I am?" If you do not yet know Him, here is a perfect opportunity to pause and ask the Holy Spirit to give you a revelation of Him. You may at this point rededicate or surrender your life to Jesus Christ, by doing the following: acknowledge that He died for you, believe in your heart that He rose on the third day, confess Him as your Lord and Saviour, and ask Him to live in your heart from now. If you prayed this prayer please contact us by email: toyin@joyfulmothers.com

TRUTHS YOU NEED TO KNOW ABOUT JESUS CHRIST

He was with God in the beginning
(Genesis 1:1-2).

"And now, O Father, glorify Me together with Yourself, with the glory which I had with You before the world was" (John 17:5).

He created all things

"All things were made through Him, and without Him nothing was made that was made" (John 1:3).

"For by Him all things were created that are in heaven and that are on earth, visible and invisible, whether thrones or dominions or principalities or powers. All things were created through Him and for Him" (Colossians 1:16).

"For of Him and through Him and to Him are all things, to whom be glory forever. Amen" (Romans 11:36).

"For everything comes from God alone. Everything lives by his power, and everything is for his glory. To him be glory evermore" (Romans 11:36, The Living Bible).

God created all things for a purpose. With Him, there are no mistakes. You were not created for you; you were created for Him. The creator lives in you. Are you in need of His creative miracle today? Is something not functioning well in your life that needs rectifying? Do you need a fibroid-free or endometriosis-free womb, patent fallopian tubes, normal level of reproductive hormones? Jesus is still in the business of healing.

He is life

"In Him was life, and the life was the light of men" (John 1:4).

In Him was life. Is there a dead area in your life? The life in Jesus Christ can resurrect your reproductive system.

"Jesus said to her, "I am the resurrection and the life. He who believes in Me, though he may die, he shall live" (John 11:25).

Those who do not have the light and life that is in Jesus Christ are in darkness and great is that darkness. As a believer, He lives in you and all you need to do is to tap into that life. Let the life in Jesus Christ give life to every dead cell which is meant to be living in you. Let the life of Jesus create the babies in your home.

He is light

"In Him was life, and the life was the light of men. And the light shines in the darkness, and the darkness did not comprehend it"
(John 1:4, 5).

The light shines in the darkness, and the darkness did not comprehend it. Are there dark areas in your life where you need God to shed more light? Is the light of Jesus shining through you in this dark world? Or are you blending with your environment. Let the light of Jesus, the Anointed One, shine in the darkest part and needy places of your life.

He is the brightness of God's glory

"Who being the brightness of His glory, the express image of Him, upholding all things by the word of His power, when He had by Himself purged our sins, sat at the right hand of the Majesty on high, having become better than angels as He has by inheritance obtained a more excellent name than they" (Hebrews 1:3-4).

Now let us carefully look at a number of elements or phrases from these 2 verses.

➢ *The brightness of His glory*

What is glory? God's glory represents, His unbelievable beauty, power and splendour (complete energy), His righteousness, perfection, holiness without blemish, goodness and love. Jesus is the brightness, lustre, glow, splendour, aroma of God.

> *"And the Word became flesh and dwelt among us, and we beheld His glory, the glory as of the only begotten of the Father, full of grace and truth"* (John 1:14).

Are you beholding His glory? When you trust in this name and take cognisance of His glory, the same brightness should be reflected through you. The brightness, lustre, glow, splendour, aroma of Jesus should also radiate through you. I pray that the lustre, glow, splendour, goodness, brightness that is in Jesus Christ will moisturise your life.

➢ *The express image of Him*

When you have seen God, you have seen Jesus Christ and vice versa.

> *"Whose minds the god of this age has blinded, who do not believe, lest the light of the gospel*

of the glory of Christ, who is the image of God, should shine on them" (2 Corinthians 4:4).

"He is the image of the invisible God, the firstborn over all creation" (Colossians 1:15).

> *Upholding all things*

Upholding (safeguarding, perpetuating) all things by the word of His power. Contrary to what the doctors say, Jesus can uphold your pregnancies to term. No more abortions or miscarriages.

"And He is before all things, and in Him all things consist" (Colossians 1:17).

Are there areas of your life that are falling apart? You need to let Jesus be at the centre of it. He is more than able to hold your life together. If infertility is taking its toll on your marriage, remember, Jesus can hold your marriage and family together. I pray that Jesus will sustain your marriage.

> *Our sins are purged*

Jesus purged our sins by Himself – not by someone else's blood, not by anything else (the blood of goats or bulls), but by His blood. By Him, our sins were purged (Hebrews 7:20-8:6).

In view of this, the guilt and shame of sin are completely broken. There is no greater love than this.

> ➤ *Sat at the right hand of the Majesty on high*

Jesus sat, not below, but on high. He is no longer on the cross. He is no longer in the grave. He is at the right hand of Majesty.

> "*The LORD said to my Lord, 'Sit at My right hand, till I make Your enemies Your footstool"* (Psalm 110:1).

> ➤ *He became so much better than angels*

Be careful of angel worship. We are in better company. Our association is with an excellent One; The Anointed One. So, we are not supposed to worship angels (Hebrews 1:4-6, 13; Revelations 22:8-9).

> "*For to which of the angels did He ever say: 'You are My Son, today I have begotten You'? And again: 'I will be to Him a Father, and He shall be to Me a Son'? But to the Son He says: 'Your throne, O God, is forever and ever; a sceptre of righteousness is the sceptre of Your kingdom'*" (Hebrews 1:5, 8).

Chapter Eight

What is in the Name 'Jesus Christ'?

Chapter Eight

What is in the Name 'Jesus Christ'?

"And she will bring forth a Son, and you shall call His name Jesus, for He will save His people from their sins. And did not know her till she had brought forth her firstborn Son. And he called His name Jesus"

(Matthew 1:21, 25).

The name 'Jesus' was given to his earthly parents by His heavenly Father. God had His plan and purpose for Jesus on earth and He chose and gave Him a name that defined the purpose.

WHAT A POWERFUL NAME WE HAVE IN JESUS CHRIST?

Recently, I read this amazing story during one of our family devotions and it touched my heart, I hope it blesses you too. "My friend wrote a letter to his newborn child that he wanted him to read when he was older: 'My dear boy, Daddy and Mummy wish that you will find and stay focused on the Light. Your Chinese name is *Xin Xuan*. *Xin* means faithfulness, contentment, and integrity; *xuan* stands for warmth and light." He and his wife carefully chose a name based on their hopes for their baby boy. ('What's in a name?'" Our Daily Bread, April 2014).

There is more to a name than we can ever imagine. Names define our lives, purpose, and who we are. If only we can all have a deeper understanding of the names we bear or call our children.

A name is the identity of every individual and creature. At creation (Genesis 1:4-8), God named everything that He created. Basically, the purpose of what He created determined the name. Furthermore, God encouraged Adam to name the beast of the field and birds of the air and he did.

""Out of the ground the LORD *God formed every beast of the field and every bird of the air, and brought them to Adam to see what he*

would call them. And whatever Adam called each living creature, that was its name. ²⁰ So Adam gave names to all cattle, to the birds of the air, and to every beast of the field. But for Adam there was not found a helper comparable to him" (Genesis 2:19-20).

It is noteworthy that the purpose of the birds and beasts could not fit for a comparable helpmeet for Adam. Therefore, no bird or beast could be referred to as woman. God had to create that helpmeet from Adam. Essentially, the name, woman, is generic. However, it coincides with her purpose in life.

"Then the rib which the LORD God had taken from man He made into a woman, and He brought her to the man. And Adam said: 'This is now bone of my bones and flesh of my flesh; she shall be called Woman, because she was taken out of Man" (Genesis 2:22-23).

We serve a God of purpose and this is exemplified in the history of creation. If an earthly father could name his child according to the purpose of that child as seen in the case of Xin Xuan, how much more would our heavenly Father.

An exploration of the name 'Jesus Christ unveiled the following: Jesus is from the Greek word Iesous pronounced (Yay-soos). This is the

Greek transliteration of the Hebrew 'Yeshua' meaning 'He shall save.' Yeshua is the shorter form of Yehoshua (Joshua) meaning "Yahweh is Salvation" (Spirit Filled Life Bible).

Christ is from the Greek word Christos pronounced as Khristoss meaning, 'the anointed one.' The root word Chrio meaning to anoint has to do with the consecration rites of a priest or king. He is a priest forever, after the order of Melchizedek. He is the reigning King.

The Hebrew meaning of Christos is Mashiyach meaning Messiah. It is argued that the transliteration of Christos into English meaning Christ deprives the word of its meaning. It is better to translate Christos in every instance as 'the anointed one' or the Messiah denoting a title. Jesus Christ means 'Jesus, the Messiah' or 'Jesus, the Anointed One, or Jesus, the Christ' therefore, emphasising that Jesus is God's Anointed One, the promised Messiah (Spirit Filled Life Bible).

What is in the name of Yeshua Mashiyach or Iesous Christos? The anointing to save, heal and deliver. What does the anointing do? The anointing destroys. I pray that the anointing in the Anointed One will flow through your reproduction and reproductive system, and it will heal and save your ovaries, spermatozoa, womb, fallopian tubes, and hormones in Jesus' name.

"How God anointed Jesus of Nazareth with the Holy Spirit and with power, who went about doing good and healing all who were oppressed by the devil, for God was with Him" (Acts 10:38).

I want you to note that Jesus of Nazareth became Jesus the Anointed One following God's anointing of Him with the Holy Spirit and power. Jesus Christ was anointed with precious and rare oil; therefore, He has the original anointing oil. This is the oil you should be tapping into, not the one in a bottle. By all means, if the one in a bottle makes more sense to you there is nothing stopping you. Jesus is the Anointed One for a purpose. May that purpose be fulfilled in your life. He will do you good, heal your reproductive organ, and deliver you from the oppression of the evil one.

The use of anointing oil in church meetings has been degraded such that people who have nothing to do with Christianity now sell it in their stores. Christians have forgotten about the anointing oil in the Anointed One. The substance in the name Iesous Christos is priceless and matchless. The anointing oil that is required to break every stronghold is in the name of Jesus Christ. As previously established in this book, Jesus is the Anointed One, and the original anointing oil is in Him.

In the name "Yeshua Mashiyach", there is fertility, healing, deliverance, salvation, His abiding presence, peace, protection, wisdom, wealth, anointing oil and much more. Many people have not yet placed a demand on the anointing that is in the name 'Jesus Christ.' I encourage you to press into the original oil.

To obtain oil from olive, you must press into it; this process takes time. But sadly, many give up too soon. It takes time and effort to get oil out of olive. So, keep pressing. The woman with the issue of blood pressed into the anointing in Jesus Christ. She placed a demand on the anointing saying, "*If I touch the hem of His garment, I shall be made whole.*" The anointing oil in Yeshua Mashiyach is still at work in contemporary times.

> "*For unto us a Child is born, unto us a Son is given; and the government will be upon His shoulder. And His name will be called Wonderful, Counselor, Mighty God, Everlasting Father, Prince of Peace*"
>
> (Isaiah 9:6).

According to these names of Jesus, the Lord will be wonderful to you and your family. He will counsel and lead you in the right direction. He will do great and mighty things in your family and give you His peace through this testing period.

HE HAS A MORE EXCELLENT NAME

There is power in His name. By inheritance, He obtained a more excellent (outstanding, superb) name. His name is the most excellent name in every situation, or circumstance. You cannot fault that name. His name is one that you can be proud to associate with. You can be confident to tender His name anywhere. His name is the most excellent treatment. I encourage you to take a dose of His name on a daily basis.

The name 'Jesus' is a name that is higher than any other name. Whatever you are currently contending with, no matter how big and scary the name may sound, it is classed as 'any other name.' No name can contend with the name of Jesus Christ. Look at infertility and miscarriages in the face, and declare they are over. Why? Because, Jesus' name supersedes their names.

"Therefore God also has highly exalted Him and given Him the name which is above every name, that at the name of Jesus every knee should bow, of those in heaven, and of those on earth, and of those under the earth, and that every tongue should confess that Jesus Christ is Lord, to the glory of God the Father" (Philippians 2:9-11).

PRAYING IN HIS NAME

As He has a more excellent name, the bible says that whatever we ask in His name will be given to us.

"And whatever you ask in My name, that I will do, that the Father may be glorified in the Son. If you ask anything in My name, I will do it" (John 14:13-14).

Prayer offered in the name of Jesus Christ has the full backing of Heaven. In my own opinion, John 14:14 is a blank Cheque. Write *whatever* you desire.

"You did not choose Me, but I chose you and appointed you that you should go and bear fruit, and that your fruit should remain, that whatever you ask the Father in My name He may give you" (John 15:16).

I want to draw your attention to the fact that you have been appointed to bear spiritual fruits as well as physical ones. Not only that, God expects that your fruit will remain. In other words, the fruits you carry in your womb are expected to remain and grow to term as well as live. God desires that we prosper both physically and spiritually; He is interested in every aspect of our lives. The scripture below buttresses this:

"Beloved, I pray that you may prosper in all things and be in health, just as your soul prospers" (3 John 2).

"Until now you have asked nothing in My name. Ask, and you will receive, that your joy may be full" (John 16:24).

A request that does not receive a seal of authentication, the name of Jesus Christ' signifies 'no prayer.' Asking must precede receiving and joy must be unleashed after receiving. Your joy will not be in small measure but in full. How are you asking? Make sure that you are asking in the name of Jesus.

Shalom!

Chapter Nine

The Blood That Speaks

Chapter Nine

The Blood That Speaks

THE POWER IN THE BLOOD OF JESUS CHRIST

once had a dream. I saw that Jesus and I were travelling the street of a city and at the same time we were deeply in conversation. He said to me, "*When people do not use the provisions that I purchased on the cross, they are wasting it.*" He shed His blood as a payment for our lives. This is His provision for mankind, and we must ensure it is carefully employed in every aspect of our lives. This dream is a reminder of how precious and useful the blood of Jesus Christ is.

Let us now explore the incomprehensible power in the blood of Jesus Christ; looking at the biblical meaning and value of blood; the fundamental history and importance of its use; as well as the power in the blood of Jesus Christ. Biblical perspectives on blood and its uses demonstrate the value that God places on human or animal blood, and that of His Son, Jesus Christ.

There is an undeniable strength in the blood of Jesus Christ. Jesus Christ entered the holy of holies once and for all as the sacrificial lamb nullifying the need for a yearly sacrifice as in the old testament. Amazingly, in our contemporary times, the provisional power in the blood of Jesus Christ is powerful enough to meet human needs.

BIBLICAL VALUE OF BLOOD

"For the life of the flesh is in the blood, and I have given it to you upon the altar to make atonement for your souls; for it is the blood that makes atonement for the soul. Therefore I say to the Israelites, 'None of you may eat blood, nor may any foreigner residing among you eat blood.' Because the life of every creature is its blood. That is why I have said to the Israelites, 'You must not eat the blood of any creature, because the life of every creature

is its blood; anyone who eats it must be cut off" (Leviticus 17:11-12, 14).

Pitching this discussion on the above scriptures, the Bible affirmatively establishes that the blood of everyone including animals is precious because, it is the life of every individual or animal.

Atonement, Forgiveness and Protection in the blood

In fact, the law requires that nearly everything be cleansed with blood, and without the shedding of blood there is no forgiveness (Hebrews 9:22).

The theme and importance of blood are carefully woven through the bible. This was demonstrated during the time of Adam and Eve following their disobedience in the Garden of Eden. In order to atone for their sins as well as cover their nakedness, the shedding of animal blood became a necessity. There is atonement, forgiveness, mercy in the blood. God can forgive the time of ignorance in your life and have mercy on you and your family.

"*But if we walk in the light as He is in the light, we have fellowship with one another, and the blood of Jesus Christ His Son cleanses us from all sin*" (I John 1:7).

"Seeing then that we have a great High Priest who has passed through the heavens, Jesus the Son of God, let us hold fast our confession. For we do not have a High Priest who cannot sympathise with our weaknesses, but was in all points tempted as we are, yet without sin. Let us therefore come boldly to the throne of grace, that we may obtain mercy and find grace to help in time of need"

(Hebrews 4:14-16).

If the blood of bulls could clean, how much more would the blood of Jesus?

Blood speaks

There was a swift change in the biblical account relating to Adam and Eve with a very short spanned progression to the issue of Cain and Abel. Cain deliberately shed his brother's blood because God accepted Abel's sacrifice over his. He committed the first murder on the face of the earth.

"Then the Lord said to Cain, "Where is Abel your brother?" He said, "I do not know. Am I my brother's keeper?" And He said, "What have you done? The voice of your brother's blood cries out to Me from the ground" (Genesis 4:9-10).

God demanded Abel's blood from Cain as Abel's blood cried to Him. Being the creator of life, God has the authority to demand the blood of others shed by us. Blood speaks, and the creator hears the cries of such blood. As if God did not know what Cain had done, He demanded from him what he had done. He gave him the opportunity to confess and repent. However, he did not.

There is blood in the hands of every individual who has engaged in abortion, or helped someone with it. Abortion is murder because it is the shedding of blood, the termination of life.

Evidence shows the following is present in a fetus at the 11th week of conception (Silent Scream 2014):

> - Heart is beating (since 18-25 days)
> - Brain waves have been recorded at 40 days
> - The baby squints, swallows, and can make a fist
> - The baby has fingerprints and can kick
> - The baby is sensitive to heat, touch, light and noise
> - The baby sucks his or her thumb
> - All body systems are working
> - The baby weighs about 1 ounce and is $2^1/_2$ to 3 inches long

> ➢ The baby could fit comfortably in the palm of your hand

The blood of the murdered one screams to God. The fetus is sensitive to touch, light, noise and heat at 11 weeks. It feels the pain during abortion and screams during the procedure, though silently. Everyone who has engaged in abortion in any way, shape or form, needs to acknowledge it and ask for God's forgiveness and cleansing.

> *"There is therefore now no condemnation to those who are in Christ Jesus, who do not walk according to the flesh, but according to the Spirit. For the law of the Spirit of life in Christ Jesus has made me free from the law of sin and death"* (Romans 8:1-2).

> *"For You formed my inward parts; You covered me in my mother's womb. I will praise You, for I am fearfully and wonderfully made; Marvelous are Your works, And that my soul knows very well. My frame was not hidden from You, When I was made in secret, And skillfully wrought in the lowest parts of the earth. Your eyes saw my substance, being yet unformed. And in Your book they all were written, The days fashioned for me, When as yet there were none of them*
> (Psalms 139:13-16).

The womb is God's laboratory, not the devil's workshop. When people carry out (permit, encourage, or support) abortion, they are turning God's laboratory into the devil's workshop. The question is, can anything good come out of the Devil's workshop? No. When God's laboratory is turned into the Devil's workshop, you can be sure there would be dire consequences. The individuals involved open themselves up to the devil as well as demonic activities, and all sorts of torments. The woman's womb becomes an altar of sacrifice for the fire god, Molech.

> *"Do not permit any of your children to be offered as a sacrifice to Molech, for you must not bring shame on the name of your God. I am The Lord"* (Leviticus 18:21, NLT).

Additionally, many people unknowingly exposed themselves to the destroyer when they deliberately engaged in abortion. If that is the case, I will advise that you consult with your pastor and seek deliverance as well as re-dedication of your womb to God. This is what the bible says,

> *"And you, being dead in your trespasses and the un-circumcision of your flesh, He has made alive together with Him, having forgiven you all trespasses, having wiped out the*

handwriting of requirements that was against us, which was contrary to us. And He has taken it out of the way, having nailed it to the cross. Having disarmed principalities and powers, He made a public spectacle of them, triumphing over them in it"

Colossians 2:13-15).

Ask for God's cleansing from every demon that might have invaded your body especially your womb. You need to forgive yourself and ensure you do not do it again.

BETTER BLOOD

Abel is a type of Jesus Christ. Jesus was killed by His own people in the same way Abel was murdered by his brother.

"To Jesus the Mediator of the new covenant, and to the blood of sprinkling that speaks better things than that of Abel" (Hebrews 12:24).

The blood of Jesus speaks better things than the blood of Abel. If Jesus' blood speaks better things, that means His blood is better. Better, in every way! If the blood of Abel could speak, how much more would the blood of Jesus Christ. Abel's blood cries for vengeance but the blood of Jesus speaks forgiveness, grace, mercy, atonement, and life.

Chapter Ten

The Protective Power in the Blood

Chapter Ten

The Protective Power in the Blood

About two years ago, I had a dream during the Resurrection period and I saw blood dropped from the sky, and landed on my roof. It was just a drop of blood. However, it completely soaked through my roof and ceiling.

The first Passover came onto the scene when the children of Israel were about to leave Egypt. The Lord passed over the Israelites because of the blood, whereas, the inhabitants of Egypt lost their first born because they were not protected by the blood. Read the full account of the institution of the Passover in Exodus 12:1-28.

'For I will pass through the land of Egypt on that night, and will strike all the firstborn in the land of Egypt, both man and beast; and against all the gods of Egypt I will execute judgment: I am the Lord. Now the blood shall be a sign for you on the houses where you are. And when I see the blood, I will pass over you; and the plague shall not be on you to destroy you when I strike the land of Egypt. For the Lord will pass through to strike the Egyptians; and when He sees the blood on the lintel and on the two doorposts, the Lord will pass over the door and not allow the destroyer to come into your houses to strike you"

(Exodus 12:12-13, 23).

The significance here is; there is protective power in the blood. Jesus Christ is now the Passover lamb and His blood can be applied over your household for protection against every form of miscarriage and stillbirths. If the blood of bulls can protect, the blood of Jesus Christ can protect much more.

"By faith he kept the Passover and the sprinkling of blood, lest he who destroyed the firstborn should touch them"

(Hebrews 11:28).

The blood of bulls was used in the first Passover and the Lord honoured it. Much more now, He would honour the blood of His only begotten Son.

Maybe the destroyer has been destroying your babies through miscarriages or abortions; the power in the blood of Jesus is available to protect you from that happening in the future. You may have been experiencing habitual abortions whereby you automatically lose your pregnancies after a period of weeks or months. Or your case might be repeated premature deliveries and stillbirths. Whatever the case, the blood of Jesus Christ has the power to protect your pregnancies and help you to deliver your babies alive.

The Biblical account about the blood carefully graduated to the Mosaic sacrifices where the blood of animals was used to cleanse and purify. This will not be discussed as it is beyond the scope of this book.

The Biblical account of the blood eventually culminated in the ultimate sacrifice of the Lamb of God when Jesus Christ was nailed to the cross and shed His precious blood at Calvary. His blood sufficiently purchased our lives from previously intended destruction. Today, there is still power in His blood.

As previously established, if the blood of human beings and animals are so precious before God, how much more is the blood of Jesus Christ.

"For if the blood of bulls and goats and the ashes of a heifer, sprinkling the unclean, sanctifies for the purifying of the flesh, how much more shall the blood of Christ, who through the eternal Spirit offered Himself without spot to God, cleanse your conscience from dead works to serve the living God?" (Hebrews 9:13-14).

THE SACRAMENT

Have communion, observe the Eucharist. Drink His blood. If the blood is the life of an individual then when you drink the blood of Jesus Christ, you are drinking His life. Jesus Christ further established this truth earlier written in Leviticus 17:11 when He said,

"Most assuredly, I say to you, unless you eat the flesh of the Son of Man and drink His blood, you have no life in you. Whoever eats My flesh and drinks My blood has eternal life, and I will raise him up at the last day. For My flesh is food indeed, and My blood is drink indeed. He who eats My flesh and drinks My blood abides in Me, and I in him. As the living Father sent Me, and I live because of the Father, so he who feeds on Me will live because of Me. This is the bread which came down from heaven — not as your fathers ate the

manna, and are dead. He who eats this bread will live forever" (John 6:53-58).

"For I received from the Lord that which I also delivered to you: that the Lord Jesus on the same night in which He was betrayed took bread; and when He had given thanks, He broke it and said, 'Take, eat; this is My body which is broken for you; do this in remembrance of Me.' In the same manner, He also took the cup after supper, saying, 'This cup is the new covenant in My blood. This do, as often as you drink it, in remembrance of Me'" (1 Corinthians 11:23-25).

HOW DO YOU DRINK HIS BLOOD?

"But let a man examine himself, and so let him eat of the bread and drink of the cup. For he who eats and drinks in an unworthy manner eats and drinks judgment to himself, not discerning the Lord's body. For this reason many are weak and sick among you, and many sleep " (1 Corinthians 11:28-30).

Christians are commanded to share the body and the blood of Jesus Christ often, as a memorial to the Lord. However, we are warned not to do it in an unworthy manner, in order not to bring self-inflicted judgement. Such judgment can be in the form of weakness, sicknesses, and death. Conversely, if the communion is observed in a worthy manner, it will bring about strength, health and life. Why not cultivate the habit of sharing communion in a worthy manner, with your spouse on a more regular basis.

VICTORY BY THE BLOOD

Finally, the book of Revelation boldly affirms that Christians overcome by the blood of the Lamb.

"And they overcame him by the blood of the Lamb and by the word of their testimony, and they did not love their lives to the death" (Revelation 12:11).

The battle over the life of your unborn children may not be a physical, but a spiritual one. The blood of Jesus Christ is a weapon you can use in collaboration with the other weapons such as the word of your testimony. The word of your testimony is what you are saying in spite of your situation. Used appropriately, victory is sure.

What an incredible journey through the blood!

Chapter Eleven

The Power of the Holy Spirit

Chapter Eleven

The Power of the Holy Spirit

"But if the Spirit of Him who raised Jesus from the dead dwells in you, He who raised Christ from the dead will also give life to your mortal bodies through His Spirit who dwells in you" (Romans 8:11).

Can you believe it? This is the question that came to mind as I began to write this chapter. The Spirit of Him who raised Jesus from the dead is the Spirit of the living God and He is still alive today. That same Spirit is called the Holy Spirit and the Bible alludes that He indwells every believer who has accepted Jesus Christ as their Lord and Saviour. Before I proceed I have another question for you. Have you received Jesus Christ as your Lord and Saviour, if you have answered 'yes' to this question, Congratulations! If you have answered 'No', this is another perfect opportunity to ask Him into your heart. All you need to do is say this prayer:

Dear Lord Jesus, I believe you are the son of God, I believe you died for my sins and purchased me with your blood. I believe you rose up on the third day and you are now seated in the right hand of majesty and you are coming back again. Come and live in my heart, and be my Lord and Saviour from now on. Fill my heart with your Holy Spirit, in Jesus name I have prayed.

If you said this prayer, congratulations! I can assure you that Jesus now lives in you, and you have the infilling of the Holy Spirit. Yes, it is that simple.

Haven't you yet learned that your body is the home of the Holy Spirit God gave you, and that he lives within you? Your own body does not belong to you"
(1 Corinthians 6:19, Living Bible).

Now when the apostles who were at Jerusalem heard that Samaria had received the word of

God, they sent Peter and John to them, who, when they had come down, prayed for them that they might receive the Holy Spirit. For as yet He had fallen upon none of them. They had only been baptized in the name of the Lord Jesus. Then they laid hands on them, and they received the Holy Spirit. And when Simon saw that through the laying on of the apostles' hands the Holy Spirit was given, he offered them money, saying, 'Give me this power also, that anyone on whom I lay hands may receive the Holy Spirit.' But Peter said to him, 'Your money perish with you, because you thought that the gift of God could be purchased with money! You have neither part nor portion in this matter, for your heart is not right in the sight of God. Repent therefore of this your wickedness, and pray God if perhaps the thought of your heart may be forgiven you'"
(Acts 8:14-22).

The power of the Holy Spirit became evident to Simon; he offered to purchase it. Peter rebuked him for his greed and stupidity. The power of the Holy Spirit is not for sale or purchase as many make it to be today. Do not be deceived, the imperishable cannot be sold or purchased with the perishable. If you fall into any of this category, you need to repent and ask for God's forgiveness.

THE HOLY SPIRIT, WHO IS HE?

Spirit is from the Greek word, 'Pneuma' meaning breath, breeze, a current of air, or wind. The word 'Pneuma' is that part of a person capable of responding to God. You also have a spirit and your spirit has the ability to respond to the quickening of the Holy Spirit. The Holy Spirit is the third person of the trinity, who draws us to Christ, convicts us of sin, enables us to accept Christ as our Lord and personal saviour, assures us of salvation, enables us to live the victorious life, understand the Bible, pray according to God's will, and share Christ with others – Word Wealth, Spirit Filled Life Bible 2002.

> *"And I will pray the Father, and He will give you another Helper, that He may abide with you forever – the Spirit of truth, whom the world cannot receive, because it neither sees Him nor knows Him; but you know Him, for He dwells with you and will be in you. I will not leave you orphans; I will come to you"* (John 14:15-18).

The word "another" in the scripture above means 'allos' in Greek. It means One besides, another of the same kind. According to Word Wealth, Spirit Filled Life Bible, the word shows similarities but diversities of operation and ministries. Jesus' use of allos for sending another comforter equals "one besides Him and in addition to Him but one just like Him. He would do in His absence what Jesus would do if He were to be physically present with you.

Jesus is our helper yet He has given us another helper. Imagine Jesus Christ sitting with you right now. What would you do? Would you continue to worry? For your information, another who is just like Jesus Christ is with you. He is the Holy Spirit. The Holy Spirit will help you in conception, He will help you to carry the pregnancy and He will help you to deliver the baby. With the Holy Spirit, your physical abilities, though weak, yet will be strengthened. The fibroid or endometriosis may have destroyed the lining of your womb yet the Holy Spirit will strengthen your womb to carry your baby to term.

THE WORK OF THE HOLY SPIRIT IN RECEIVING YOUR MIRACLE

"Now the birth of Jesus Christ was as follows: After His mother Mary was betrothed to Joseph, before they came together, she was found with child of the Holy Spirit"
(Matthew 1:18).

Without any shadow of doubts, there will never be another virgin pregnancy or birth. That said, the Holy Spirit is still in the business of making babies.

Three days following Jesus' death and burial, the Holy Spirit performed a spectacular and awesome miracle. He raised Jesus from the dead. The scripture in Romans 8:11 indicates that if that same Spirit indwells us, He will also give life to our mortal bodies. The truth is that the Holy Spirit indwells us and He remains alive, effective and efficient. He is there to give life to your body, womb, and hormones. In fact, the Holy Spirit is able to infuse life to every part of your body that may be dead, or non-functional. He is alive to correct every structural deformity in your body.

The Holy Spirit brought Jesus back to life. He is still available to do the same in you and bring every dead organ in your body back to life. You can also release your body to the Holy Spirit and let Him do His work of quickening, restoration and renewal. He is the only One who knows what tissue or cells that needs to be restored and He certainly is able to reach every part of your body in need of a touch. Not only that, He is the breath of life and He has the power to infuse the appropriate organ and ensure its resurrection. May be you have had several explainable or unexplainable miscarriages or still births, you must now allow your spirit to connect with the life-giving-power in the Holy Spirit Who will ultimately bring about a new life at the end of nine months. It is a new day, and a new dawn in your life and family. Receive it, if you believe it.

Conclusion

The Truth about Jesus Christ

His name is higher than any other name
His blood is better than any other blood
His word is greater than any other word

There is life in the blood of Jesus
There is life in the name of Jesus
There is life in the word of Jesus

There is power in the name of Jesus
There is power in the blood of Jesus
There is power in the word of Jesus

There is life in the Spirit of Jesus Christ
The Word of God is Jesus and He is life
The blood of Jesus is His life
Jesus is life
The Holy Spirit of Jesus gives life

What more can we ever ask for?

It is not a coincidence that there is life in the Word, the name of Jesus, His blood, and the Holy Spirit. Certainly, not an accident! If you need to make life then cling to the life in Jesus Christ.

OTHER BOOKS BY THE AUTHOR

- ➢ Joyful Mother of Children
- ➢ 40 Days of Power – Daily Devotional for Waiting Couples

www.ingramcontent.com/pod-product-compliance
Lightning Source LLC
Chambersburg PA
CBHW071547040426
42452CB00008B/1103